pictureshowpress.net

Some of the poems in this book were previously published in the following places. Thank you to their editors for making them a home: *Boston Accent Lit* ("Lunch Break"); *Horny Poetry Review* ("Below Into the Deep" and "Calendar Girls"); *Rose Quartz Magazine* ("Breathing Still," "My Sex Ed.," "Sex, a Place," and "Some Days"); and *V: An Anthology of Poetry* ("The Gun on the Nightstand" and "Vixen").

Cover art: Rachel Brodsky

FIRST EDITION

ISBN-13: 978-1-7324144-7-1
ISBN-10: 1-7324144-7-5

Quiver

a sexploration

POEMS BY
HOLLY PELESKY

Picture Show Press

POEMS

1   Calendar Girls

3   My Sex Ed.

4   Breathing Still

5   The Gun on the Nightstand

6   Below Into the Deep

8   To the Lover I Never Had

9   Vixen

10   Shapes We Make

12   Lunch Break

13   Some Days

14   Making Love

15   Sex, a Place

16   Every Season is Mating Season

18   When My Body Thinks for Me

19   Good for Something

20   When I Say

25   Or Maybe

Calendar Girls

I am twelve when
my sister and I peer into the windows of
my father's Eagle Talon hatchback
parked in the driveway, locked.
The windows
aren't tinted because that costs extra.
It is clean inside, empty
except for a calendar of sexy women in bikinis.

I say sexy now
but then
I didn't know what that meant.
I knew that mothers
were married to fathers,
but I didn't know about desire:
about holes that need filling,
tension that needs releasing.
I didn't know the euphoria of orgasm,
how we chase it like a drug, taking hit
after hit after hit after hit.

Then I only knew that my dad had
half naked women locked
away in his car.
I wiggled the door handle.
Maybe he had forgotten.
He hadn't.
I tried the passenger door,
but it was also locked.

I thought of where the keys could be,
if I could sneak them when my sister left,
climb inside that car,
sweat in that hot stale air,

so tight and contained,
the sun beating through the unprotected windows,
flipping past January to
February, March, April, May.

My Sex Ed.

When "masticate" was a vocabulary word,
the whole class snickered; everyone, but me.
"To chew," I announced, the only raised hand.

When I first wore a sanitary pad, I wore two
taped against my legs at a soccer game
when I forgot my shin guards.

When a girl in my dorm explained how sex works,
she said the penis goes inside your vagina,
not between your lower lips like a hot dog in a bun.
"Ouch!" my friend and I squealed in
unison or what felt like unison.

When I thought I was ready to "do it,"
when I wanted to be touched, knew
I could feel loved that way, I spent
an hour at the public library with
sex books hidden inside encyclopedias,
trying to catch up on all I had missed,
blushing, laying my elbow
across the page
when anyone walked by.

Yet
when I lost
my virginity,
I knew better
than to look for it
under the bed.

Breathing Still

The first time I slept next to a body that wasn't my sister's,
I didn't take off my coat. My gray wool coat, so long
it covered my ass because that's how you manage through
winters here in Nebraska. I was sweating an unholy amount
at my first boyfriend's house on his bed without
a headboard or footboard that wasn't against a wall, just
drifting in the middle of the room like a raft.

When his body was next to mine, I listened
to his breathing, waited for it to thicken so I
could stop worrying that he would touch me.
"You can take your coat off," he said
and I said, "I'm fine. I'm not even hot," although
no doubt he smelled my armpits through the wool.

I listened to a clock tick in the other room and worried
his roommate with the shiny shirt and the samurai sword would
walk in and make lewd eyes and ask if we had banged yet and
worried, mostly, about what my mother would say if she ever
found out. I lay there, still as a corpse, cursing myself
for this knack I had of putting myself at the mercy of a man,
daring not to move until I thought he was asleep.
Then I pushed my thick sleeves up to my elbow, hoping
he wouldn't wake at the sound and touch me at
dreaded last, that I could stay
afloat a while longer, breathing still.

The Gun on the Nightstand

I didn't lose my virginity
as much as I surrendered it.
The gun on the nightstand
whispered to me through its
cold barrel, *stay afraid* so I
lay still, blood wet beneath
me, staining his sheets, soaking
the air in a coppery sour, stitching
my mouth into silence, keeping my
feet from my shoes.

Below Into the Deep

I am indestructible.
You think that means
I *can* not be destroyed,
but it means that I
will not be destroyed.

Last November, when drunk
(but not because of it),
I almost fell in when a girl kissed me.
Her tongue traced circles around mine,
mulled me over. Her hands were soft,
but firm; she pulled my face into hers,
an abyss if I let it swallow me.

I followed her
into the bathroom at Vagabonds;
she fingered me in the handicap stall, me
backed up against a Sharpied "fuck Matt."
I had never liquefied like that, never orgasmed
so quickly. She pressed her number into my hand,
scrawled on a wet BevNap.

I think her name was Kate,
maybe it was Kara.
I never called her, although I wanted to.
I still feel her breath, hot in my ear,
reverberating through me.

I returned to my firm, rigid seat,
beside this man who claimed me.
He reached for my hand, interlaced
my fingers with his, filling up my space,
squeezing it out of me. He asked,
"Are you OK?" and I bit my lip,

my tongue. I nodded.
His nails dug into my skin.

I want to be bad for good,
but being indestructible
means *don't self-destruct.*

When I learned I was pregnant
with his baby, this man with the claws,
I nibbled the inside of my cheek while
I waited on hold with the clinic,
calm music playing like a command.
When he got home: "How was your day?"
I shook the newspaper like it was
just another one, a Monday with a high
of 55. My tongue was raw.

I hid the clinic handout
underneath the tire below my trunk,
undiscoverable—this secret me.

Standing on a bridge above dark,
choppy water, I shredded those words
that soothed and pained: words about living
after life has been sucked from your body.
I tossed them below into the deep.
I decided not to jump.

To the Lover I Never Had

You don't know I keep my socks on in bed;
I haven't licked the mole on your lower back
you're trying to remove with apple cider
vinegar. I don't know your sweat smells
like a bike seat left in the rain; you haven't
watched me persuade my body into a lacy
bodysuit with a snap crotch before.

I didn't twirl with your long charcoal black
hair while you told me how it was to
grow up in a big family, in that crowded split-
level. Didn't twist it on my finger while you said
you haven't grown up all the way, called me
your adolescent lover although we're in our thirties.

I bet I would've wiped the love juice you left on
my face off with my hand, licked my hand clean;
I bet after you left I would've smelled my sour sheets
like a fiend; I bet you would've burbled soft
snores when you slept and I bet I would've watched
your chest rise and fall, bet I would've pressed a palm
into your breast to feel your heart beat beat beat.

If we would've loved it could've
been fitful and urgent or slow
and serene or frantic and exhausting
or secretive and brief. Whatever it was,
it would've been love of a sort, and maybe
you'd be better for it or maybe I am better
like this, wanting to pull a lock of your
hair into my wet mouth, suck the flavor
you place in this outstretched spoon.

Vixen

It isn't hard to find a lover,
only to keep one.

Once he says *I love you*,
I smile, hold his hand, drop
my head into the dip
of his shoulder.

Never do I love him back.

I zip into his adoration, let it
cradle me for awhile.
Let it hold me in tight, warm
against its bosom, as if I belong
somewhere.

Then,
I drop out—when
the man confusing me with love
smells like sweat again, no longer
sweet like infatuation.

This is how I leave them: goose bumped,
shaky, an unlit cigarette between clenched teeth,
wondering why I can't give love like a smile.

Shapes We Make

When sex was an
arrow pointed at my
womb, it threatened
me with a life I didn't
want, one with fingernails.

When I quivered, it was
fear of the arrow, not
desire to hold it.

I never wanted to
sheath a weapon
which could pierce
a tunnel into me,
swell my insides
around a body.

I know what an arrow
does to a body when
it's removed: how
it tears flesh inside
out, blood streaming
down legs in rivulets.

Before I touched a woman
I fucked a man with
eyes closed, envisioned
her body above mine:
orbed breasts inside
empty cups I held as hands.

I let him plunge a deep
void where dread lived,
turn my fear into bodies,

sad babies that lived
in the sheets between us.

When I fucked a woman
no shaft thrust inside
me spilling my blood
on the sheets, no empty eyes
looking up at me from the dark.

Instead of coarse whiskers
breaking a rash above my lips,
when I remembered
how to be
unafraid
her soft skin kissed mine
to music that curves
hips into figure eights.

Lunch Break

I had an emotional affair.
Someone took an interest in me
the way I wanted—
in the daily changes way,
not the one-time infatuation way.

We went to a mall on lunch break
to pick up the ring for his fiancée.
Our jeweler confused me for her.
We didn't correct him. We ate Sbarros.

Some Days

the sad beats
out the sex and then we lie
in bed silently, touching
vaguely, distractedly: an
arm over a stomach maybe,
a toe resting against a foot.
We stare at our arms or the ceiling,
anything but each other, afraid of
what we are without our bodies.

Making Love

Your hand lost in my hair, not looking for
a way out; two eyes consuming my body in hungry
want; the scent of your lust (thick, hot,
peppery); our voices husky and then light and then husky
again; your tongue soft and gentle on my neck;
teeth tenacious in the same spot; my hands
rub up your thighs to the place that makes you
shiver, how you shiver, how I shiver, when I bury
my face there—you smell like something wheaty and
decadent I can't place—now your arm drapes over my side
tenderly like it belongs, like I belong. I know we said
this is only fucking, but it feels like
a recipe I don't have, I just remember what
it made: a tart that melted in my mouth, made me
ravenous for its sweet then sour.

Sex, a Place

With tangled legs and intertwined fingers
we build a fort, make sex a place.
Our hands roam up legs, stomachs; down necks, breasts.
Our fingers grip sheets, skin, hair in fistfuls.
Our tongues thrust into warm spaces: lick lips, ridges, valleys.

We play, naked: clothes heaped on the ground.
We flood our senses: fingers moaning for more
to trace, grip, graze, tongues clutching up flavors,
mouths listening, warm, hungry. Soft light shadowing
hipbones, skin shivering at the taste of touch.
The sheets smell like us, the moist between our legs.

We pack our place with us, carry it; our reprieve
we pitch against trees, in backseats, behind doors.
Between the gym and the dentist, or early morning,
or in the dark of night when the dew is settling in,
we return, gaping again, to this place only we can make.

Every Season is Mating Season

When it rains, I want to stand outside
with you and no umbrella, feel the cold
drops prickle my skin while you lay your
head on my shoulder, while I stroke your hair.
You will wink and say "You know what else is wet"
without the question mark and I'll laugh and
we will sing songs from movies into the heavy clouds
and it will feel like only we and the rain exist.
After a long while we will move inside where the
kettle will whistle while your tongue is in
my mouth, while my hair leaves streaks
across your cheeks, while we make jokes
of creating our own steam.

When the sun throbs through my windshield,
I want to drive with no destination, eating
Jack-in-the-Box tacos, lettuce shreds all
over my lap, singing loudly to the pop songs
on the radio, holding your hand across
the console, giggling into the warm air that
breezes across our faces from the open windows.
We will find an empty park and walk—your hand
down my skirt, on my ass—to the dugout where
you'll say, "There's something I want to dig out,
knowwhatI'msayin'?" and I'll smile and push
you onto the bench, straddle you, stick my
breast to your mouth, watch you suck, my nipple
hardening while I sweat onto your bare thighs.

When it turns cool, I want to read to you,
doing the voices so you know who's speaking
without seeing the page. My hand will be tracing
circles and squares and triangles on your palm.
When your stomach rumbles, I will make us

sandwiches, cut diagonally. Then we will
drag sleeping bags outside and fall
asleep under the stars to a tune we both hear
although no music is playing.

When the snow packs hard like dirt on the ground,
I want to go sledding with a garbage can lid
since neither of us owns a sled. I will climb
on it behind you, my legs spread. At the
bottom of the hill, when our hair is windblown,
our noses red, our lips chapped, you will turn to me
and warm your numb hands in my scarf and
I will guide them into my coat and you will say,
"I know how we can warm up" and we will slide
just once more down the hill and then return
to my home, to the whistling kettle, to peeling
off our wet clothes, to steam and how to make it.

When My Body Thinks for Me

it wonders over your skin, the smooth of your
cheeks, the prickle of the hair on the back of your neck. It ponders
between your toes, up your calves, behind
your knees, mulls through your thighs.
Touch with a brain of its own listening to writhing, gripping,
suspension. Speaking in moans I didn't know I make. When my
skin smelled yours, it had
to taste you, hold you on my tongue.
Do you know the antonym of *sensual*?
Neither do I, not right now. My head's brain only works in
carnal solitude, after you remind me what it is to inhabit
a body, how to wear skin and let it speak, react.

Then
I return to my slow breathing, heavy
thinking, endless exploration of words
while my skin hangs on a rod, untouched.

Good for Something

I like the way sex smells: like butternut squash pooled on concrete.
I like wearing it on myself throughout my errands—
the bank and the grocery store and the post office—
wafting in and out of places with our lust between my legs.

During sex I feel the most useful, wanted, good for
something. I have never seamlessly slipped
into the world, but rather, I've felt the space
I took up in it, the weight of me. But when some
one heaves and shudders against my touch, when
a mouth bites my shoulder, when a voice screams my
name in euphoria, I am weightless, floating
above time and space, oblivious to my place
in the world, if I have one or don't.

It is with this whiff of usefulness
that I go about my day, filled to the brim
like my morning coffee which I drink
as a dog would, head bent over, greedily lapping.

When I Say

I want you to fuck me so hard
I can't think anymore, I mean it; I do.
I want you to bend me over something, anything:
a table,
a car's trunk,
one of those giant rocks that teenagers graffiti their names onto
and then I want you to slip two of your strong, nimble fingers
into me where I'm wet, under my skirt
—I'm not wearing any underwear—
I want you to swirl one finger, pulsate the other
while you pull my hair and tell me
I'm a dirty slut, your breath hot in my ear
if you can manage the angle.

I want my failed relationships,
my disappointed parents,
my retail job, my underachieving,
my incessant self-loathing
to disappear into the gray static
when I cum.

But when I say I want that, I also mean something else.

I mean I want to make you hot chocolate afterward,
topped high with whip cream from a can.
I want to wipe it off your top lip with my thumb,
make silly, immature jokes about guzzling cum.
I want to listen to oldies while piecing
together a puzzle with you there,
trying aimlessly to figure out the difference between
an edge piece and a middle piece or
reading a book or twirling
your hair for all I care.
If you're reading, read it aloud to me, a book

we both love. Don't read it dryly.
But do say that nothing is dry when we're together.
Say it with an exaggerated wink or a laugh
that sounds like wind chimes.
I'll part your hair when it falls into your face;
tuck it behind your ear.

Tell me about your grandmother,
about the wind chimes on her back porch,
how her house smelled like raspberries or bell peppers or cow
    manure.
Tell me what an awkward kid you were,
how you were always alone:
running around naked in a pasture
or stealing ring pops from a convenience store or
licking your mother's postage stamps for the taste.
Look at childhood pictures with me.
Laugh at our mullets and colorful windbreakers.
Wonder aloud if we would've liked each other had we
known one another back then.
We will, of course, agree:
we wouldn't have. I'm lucky to be spared
that early version: that little shit.
And I would've been too uncool to be your friend.

When I say I want to fuck you I also mean
I want you to take me out to dinner.
I'll drive.
I want you to feed me bread dipped in olive oil and parmesan:
guide it into my mouth with your hand and let me lick your fingers.
I want you to run your foot up my leg under the table.
I want us both to flirt with the waitress.
I want to stare at your face while my mouth is on my straw,
watch your eyes move across the menu,
watch you make up your mind. I will say,
"You're no one-minute man," and you will laugh so heartily,
so hard that you blow out the candle in the middle

of the table. Make a silly, immature quip about blowjobs.
If you don't, I will.
When the waitress reappears, let her decide
what you'll eat. When the bill comes, slip your
credit card into the book so stealthily that
I can't see how much it costs.
I will be adding it up in my head.
You will say, "Stop calculating."
I'll say, "But I'm very calculating."
Then I'll bite my lip or lick it and you
will shudder and say, "Let's go home," which is a slip up,
it's actually my place,
but I don't mind,
I actually like it.
That's the hottest thing I've heard all day, and earlier
you called me a dirty slut while you
finger fucked me over a graffitied rock.

Fuck me again, but more tenderly.
Grip my ears with your hands, rub
your thumbs down the back of my lobes. Lick
my neck, then down and up the slopes of me:
my breasts, my hip bones, my thighs.
Tell me you love my body.
I'll say, "Of course," like
I have the world's most perfect one.
Then say, "But it's not just that,
I love your mind too."
I'll squirm there,
writhe really.
Then I will pull
your mouth into mine, lick
the inside of your top lip
until you arm hairs stand
on end.

After we fuck, and this is important,
the most important thing:
spoon me.
First dress into ratty sweats and a t-shirt or don't.
Brush your teeth or don't.
But under no circumstances should you
put on shoes. Because when I say
I want you to fuck me, what I really mean
is I want you to hold me.

I want you to drape one arm over
my torso while resting your other hand on
my pillow, stroking my hair.
If you have an early meeting, set an early alarm.
But don't you dare sit at the edge of the bed and measure
my breathing until I fall asleep and then slip out.
You must know this.
You must.

When I say I want to see you naked
what I really mean is I want to see you
exposed. I want to hear you sing aloud
or adopt an accent or watch you dance in place.
I want to see you comfortable.

When I say I want you to fuck me
I mean I want you to mind fuck me:
get so close to me I believe
I'm loveable still. Make me question
if anything I believe is true at all.
Make me spin, twirl, sway, dip
until I'm so dizzy that I forget who I was,
gray static, swirling in my head so it feels
like I'm cumming when I'm not because
companionship is the only thing I've ever
wanted, I've just dressed my want in slutty clothes.

I work up some inexplicable courage beneath
the lump in my throat and walk
up to you at that table by the window and say,
"Want to share a post-coital cigarette?"
even though I don't smoke and by the looks of it,
neither do you, but if you're the right
kind of person, you'll know exactly what I mean.

Or Maybe

I have it all wrong, thinking
the body and the brain separate.

Doesn't my skin ripple
to the words
in your voice? Doesn't my
cerebrum quake
when you take off
your gloves?

When your hair falls
through my fingers, my
mind wavers. I feel you
in the grooves of my
elbows, the pockets
of my skull.

Our thirst
envelops the
cleft
between senses
into the gray
matter, into
the folds of our skin.

ACKNOWLEDGMENTS

Thank you to Shannon Phillips for believing in the words I hadn't yet written.

And to Teri Youmans Grimm for your cheerleading and thoughtful suggestions.

And to Kate Gale for telling me to write sex in the first place.

And to my writing group: Jen, Colleen, Joel, and Barry. I am lucky to keep such indulgent company, to sharpen writing skills with such talented friends.

Finally, to my orange half, my muse. For choosing to share time with me. To say I am grateful would be less than enough.

Holly Pelesky is a lover of spreadsheets, giant sandwiches, and handwritten letters. She holds an MFA from the University of Nebraska. She cobbles together gigs to get by, refusing to give up this writing life. She lives in Nebraska with her two sons.

Rachel Brodsky enjoys the reckless pursuits of new ideas, and taking off on last-minute road trips. She is an artist and hairstylist, and holds a Bachelor of Science in Neuroscience from the University of Nebraska. She currently lives in Omaha, Nebraska.